And Heaven Stood Silent...

Christopher C Billiot

And Heaven Stood Silent...

Christopher C. Billiot

Kravitz & Sons

INNOVATORS IN PUBLISHING, MARKETING AND ADVERTISING

Kravitz and Sons LLC
1301 Farmville Blvd, Suite 104
Greenville, NC 27834

Published by Kravitz and Sons LLC.
ISBN: 979-8-89639-704-5 (sc)
ISBN: 979-8-89639-703-8 (e)

Library of Congress Control Number: TO FOLLOW

Dedication

This book is dedicated to my parents, the late Anthony C. Billiot and Dorothy Lovell Billiot, who loved me and set a good example for me over the years.

This book is also dedicated to my son, Aaron C. Billiot, of whom I am so proud. Also dedicated to my siblings Maggie, Sonia, Craig, Bryant and my late sister Rhonda.

My wife Shelly and my grand-children Miaah, Landon and Emme.

It was a bitter, cold December night. The wind howled through the trees as the arctic air blew with the fierceness of a hurricane. Storm clouds gathered on the horizon as the forces of good and evil were about to collide. With the occasional lull in the tempest, I could hear the incessant howling of a lone wolf and the foreboding hoot of a wise owl (sentries on their post) as they warned both man and beast alike about the creatures on the move this bitter, cold evening.

While mortal men slept, totally oblivious to the warnings and movements of creatures not of the realm of man, one person was called upon to witness and intercede in the drama about to unfold, a drama unknown to mortal man, but one forever logged in the annals of the highest courts of the heavenly realms.

Perhaps it was the rhythmic tap, tap, tap of the shutters as they fell prey to the howling wind; or maybe it was the piercing howls of the wolf or the eerie hooting of the owl that seemed to beckon to me and warn me to be vigilant on this cold winter's night. Whatever the cause for my insomnia, I lay restless in my bed, unable to sleep.

Suddenly, I felt compelled to rise and look out the window of my second story apartment. As snow covered the rooftops and landscapes alike, pure white crystals glistened beautifully with a silver}' glow as a full moon cast its magic everywhere.

Taking in the wondrous beauty of the moment, I glanced down to notice a humble, homely-looking cottage like one you'd find in a fairytale. As I looked through the cottage's frost-covered window, a picture-perfect scene caught my eye.

The dim glow of a candle cast its shadow across one of the rooms, creating a silhouette of two small children as they knelt beside their bed, their little hands cupped together in prayer. One was a boy, and the other a girl.

Gazing at the pure innocence of that precious sight, I suddenly felt unattached from the reality of the moment. Feeling overwhelmed and as though I was going to faint, I closed my eyes for a brief second, hoping it would help my mind to focus.

When I opened my eyes, the quaint little cottage no longer was in view. Instead appeared a strange breath-taking scene, almost indescribable to the mortal mind. In that brief moment when I closed my eyes, I'd been whisked away (in the spirit or in the body, I could not tell) to a place of untold beauty and majesty.

I found myself in what appeared to be the very' presence of the holy angels and the Father himself. Yes 1 d been ushered into the very throne room of God. I couldn't make out much of the activity going on.

Then I noticed a most beautiful being, which I figured to be an angel, coming towards me. He was huge by human standards, his sculpted features and deep piercing eyes revealing the strength he possessed. With a commanding voice no mortal could ever imitate, he introduced himself as Raphael, my guide and my servant.

"You are my servant?" I questioned.

He replied, "Those who are washed in the blood are heirs of such a great inheritance that even the angels shall be subject to them.

Together we stood on a balcony. Gathered on the pavilion below were magnificent, powerful winged steeds, such as the legendary Pegasus. Attending each of these stallions was a gathering of beings wearing pure white robes.

When I asked my guide who they were, he replied, "They are the saints of The Most High God. These heirs of salvation." he said, "are preparing their steeds for a most special day."

At the head of this most august assembly stood a person I could hardly look upon because of the radiance oi his very being. I knew he must be the Lord of heaven and earth.

I could see on another balcony an angel of great stature and fierceness of countenance blowing a golden trumpet. My guide informed me that this was the angel Gabriel.

I then observed a gigantic, golden scale of balance, much like the well known scale of justice. This golden scale was fixed in a room which appeared to be the center of a hub with portals fanning in all directions. Angelic beings representing each nation were arriving through the portals. Each angel carried a tally-like book they handed to those angels attending the scale.

I asked my guide about this.

"Watch closely," he advised. "You are here to witness an event of unprecedented importance that the church should know about."

As each nation was called and an angel came forth, I again asked my guide the meaning of this scene.

He replied, "As the nations are called, the tallies affect the balance of the scale."

Raphael further elaborated, "The left side of the scale represents judgement for the nations, the appointed time of deliverance for the church, and the numerous sins of each nation. The right side represents the prayers of the saints."

Raphael added. "The fate of mankind is about to meet a juncture in time. And you have been chosen to witness this great juncture."

He continued, "The balance has always been in favor of the right side of the scale from the beginning of the nations because the prayers of the saints have always outweighed those nations' sins. However, within the last century, the balance has started shifting. The sins of mankind are beginning to outweigh the saints' prayers of intercession, and these prayers are losing their advantage."

Raphael commented on how at one point in mankind's history, the saints' intercessory prayers had dwindled so much that the balance was on the verge of shifting. When mankind was about to face its darkest hour, the Father intervened by creating the church, whose main purpose is for intercession, chiefly by prayer.

For the last two thousand years, the scale has been in favor of man. However, it has been slowly shifting towards judgement. Raphael explained that the fate of mankind was hanging by a delicate balance that could shift at any moment, which is the reason for all the activity I was witnessing.

As the angels continued to enter one by one to give an account of the nations, 1 asked, "What about my beloved country, America?"

Raphael replied, "America is represented by the angel fondly called Lady Liberty. America has always had a special place in the Father's heart because she has carried the brunt of the evangelistic ministry. She is a nation of "mini-Jesuses" as the father fondly calls America's saints. The Father knows America can be counted on to keep the balance shifted in favor of mankind."

At that very moment, the arrival of the angel of China was announced. Approaching the angels attending the scale, the angel of China handed them a tally sheet.

Raphael then spoke to the attending angels in a heavenly language incomprehensible to mortal ears. As the angels looked toward me, they read the tally sheets before setting them onto the plate of the scale.

It was then that I fully understood what was taking place.

The attending angels read aloud:

"10,000 abortions in China today,

5,000 divorces in China today,

1,500 murders in China today..."

After reading aloud the other heinous sins of the nation, the angels paused. All of heaven stood silent.

The faces of these majestic creatures revealed both the anguish and the sorrow of what was unfolding before my very eyes. As I looked at the Father, my heart felt heavy. Tears flowed from my eyes. My spirit grieved with sorrow seeing His sadness.

Then the attending angels read aloud,

"0 prayers offered in China today."

A great hush swept over the entire realm of heaven. The scale delicately teetered on a perfect balance. The tally sheets were then tossed into the plates, causing a shifting of the scale. For what seemed an eternity, the left plate slowly eased down in favor of judgement, offsetting that delicate balance.

Then up went the plate again. I heard "ooh's as the right side slowly eased down in favor of man. As the right plate reached its lowest level, a sign of relief was heard throughout the throne room. But then the right side started moving back up again. All eyes remained fixed on the scale. Up past the balance point, the right plate continued ever so slowly, causing the left side to move slowly downward. I could fee the intensity of the moment in the courts of heaven as the left plate eased down toward the balance point again.

The inevitable was about to take place. This day and hour would be remembered throughout eternity as mankind's judgment was about to be pronounced. The hosts of heaven bowed their heads as the saints mounted their glorious steeds along with the Lord of Heaven and Earth. My heart felt lodged in my throat.

With divine wisdom and understanding, Raphael explained this as a time of great joy for the church. The Father would be gathering His children home. But this would also be a sorrowful day for those who refused the Father's greatest act of love shown them through the suffering and death of His precious son. They would be left behind.

As the saints mounted their anxious steeds and Gabriel put his golden trumpet to his lips. Jesus took hold of the bridles of His magnificent winged stallion and turned to look back at the Father asking. "Father, is it time?

13

The Father slowly rose from His throne with His head bowed low, seeming to take an eternity to reach a full upright position. The endless wars of man and the innocent victims of such, the tally of senseless abortions, (sacrifices upon the Alter of Convenience), around the world strengthened his resolve to put an end to the depraved antics of the human race. He desired to avenge those poor, helpless little souls who had not asked to be brought into a cold, loveless world. At that very moment, all eyes turned toward the scale. The left plate tilted downward, sealing the fate of all mankind.

Raphael suddenly asked the attending angels, "Has Lady Liberty reported in today?"

The angels slowly shook their heads, "No!"

As the Father raised His arms upward, He hesitantly began to give the command, "It is time..."

Then he paused... In His infinite wisdom and omniscience, He knew there was hope. All was not lost.

During that pause, a silence fell over the entire throne room of heaven. The silence lingered for what seemed an eternity. All present stood in dreaded anticipation of the Father's next words. "Go! Bring my children home." With these orders, the most breathtaking assembly of beings would ride off and forever change the course of history for mortal men and even heaven itself.

I thought to myself. *Surely, in all of America, someone must be praying. Surely, there are prayers being lifted up by the faithful.*

My thoughts immediately went to that little cottage and the two small children kneeling in prayer. As soon as these thoughts entered my mind. Raphael quickly turned towards me. At that moment, I knew these angelic creatures possessed the ability to read the thoughts of mortal men.

Just as quickly as he glanced my way, Raphael walked over to the Father and held a private conversation with an occasional glance towards me.

The Father suddenly stood up, announcing with a thunderous voice, **"We must summon Lady Liberty!!!"** Then He raised his hands and placed them on His temple. Holding His arms in a horizontal position. He closed His eyes.

Blinding lightning flashed. Thunder pealed with such magnitude as to make the fielded artillery of the battle fields of man pale by comparison. The foundations of heaven shook.

The voice of Lady Liberty broke through the thunder, **"Yes, Father, have you summoned me?"**

"Yes, Lady Liberty, make haste. Scour the land of the saints and bring back to me their prayers. But the prayers must be from the purest of hearts. Go quickly. The fate of Man hangs in the balance."

Once again the blinding lightning flashed, and the deafening thunder pealed. All of heaven prayed that Lady Liberty would not let mankind down. At that moment, I did not think this would be so difficult a task.

It was then that Raphael spoke to me of the graveness of the situation saying, "America was from the beginning of her establishment, the Father's pride and joy because of her steadfast love for the gospel. But in the last century. Americans have grown complacent. They have given up that love for the deceitfulness of riches. And because of the great blessings bestowed upon them. Americans have grown haughty with pride, thinking in their hearts they do not need God. During the last few generations, the torch has not been borne as in previous generations. Although America is rich with many of the most beautiful churches in the realm of man and her people go to those churches looking beautiful on the outside, their hearts have become proud and their souls defiled because of their arrogance. And so it is no longer from a pure heart that their prayers are lifted to heaven."

I felt such sorrow, such heaviness of heart for my beloved country. I stood helpless before this august assembly of the most holy of creatures, fearing the fate of mankind was about to be sealed as the left side of the scale started to reach its lowest extreme. I feared Lady Liberty would be too late to stop the tragedy before us.

As the Father slowly rose from his majestic throne with the saddest of eyes, I cried as He lifted his head towards the mounted saints. He hesitantly raised his arms in gesture.

Suddenly, a distant voice shouted from the portals, faintly at first but growing louder, ***"Stop! Wait! Not Yet! Stop! Wait! Not Yet!"***

Lady Liberty emerged into the throne room holding a tally sheet in her hand. She quickly moved towards the Father and handed it to Him. Just as the left side of the scale reached its most crucial point, the Father quickly looked at the tally sheet, handed it back to Lady Liberty, and made a gesture to toss the sheet unto the scale. As the tally sheet landed onto the right side of the scale, the balance began to shift in favor of man. The Father bowed His head for a moment. Then He raised it again.

Time may have stood still for only a few brief moments between the time the Father began to utter marching orders to His son and the moment Lady Liberty handed the tally sheet to the Father. But in those brief moments, as the weight of the sins of mankind seemed to outweigh the prayers of the saints, a prayer from the purest of hearts shifted the balance in favor of man. America had come through once again.

Shouts of **"Hooray!"** reverberated throughout the entire realm of heaven as the Father announced. ***"Not now, Son, it is not time yet! There is still one little girl praying for her daddy. There is still one little boy praying for his mommy."***

And in the twinkling of an eye, I suddenly found myself baek in my second story apartment, standing at the window looking down at the sight of two precious angels, a little boy and a little girl kneeling in prayer beside their bed.

With a river of tears and a heavy heart, I knelt on the floor and began to pray, **"Lord, please have mercy on America, please bless the little children."**

Christopher C. Billiot

About The Author / About The Story

Christopher Billiot is a Native American, born and raised in the small South Louisiana fishing town of Dulac, Louisiana, where he grew up hunting and fishing in the many beautiful swamps and bayous of the area. A graduate of South Terrebonne High School in Bourg, Louisiana, reared in the Catholic faith, Chris now attends Grand Caillou Baptist Church and is actively involved in ministry work, including teaching Sunday school.

Chris is a captain on inshore and offshore vessels servicing the oilfields in the Gulf of Mexico and inland waterways of the Gulf Coast. And Heaven Stood Silent.,, came to Chris in the wee hours of the morning at approximately 2:00 a.m. during the summer of 2001. At the time, Chris was navigating the inland waterways of the Morgan City, Louisiana, area as captain of the Aqua Eagle.

Thinking the story was very powerful, Chris felt he should write it on paper. He scribbled a few notes that morning, then pushed the story onto a backburner in his mind thinking surely everyone has these moments of inspiration.

Committing the story to memory, Chris paid no further attention to it.

Approximately a year later Chris met a truck driver who said he was a pastor in the Baton Rouge area. The truck driver/pastor said he hosted a radio program that ministered to a dozen or so parishes. Immediately upon hearing of the radio program, Chris thought it would be an excellent place for exposure for his story. So Chris mentioned to his new found friend (whom he nicknamed Rev.) that he had a story the Lord had given him. If Rev. had time, Chris would tell him the story.

The story so stunned Rev. that he was speechless for a minute or two, hardly blinking an eye as he stared at and past Chris. It was then that Chris realized the powerful impact the story had on people and decided to put it in writing to be shared with the world.

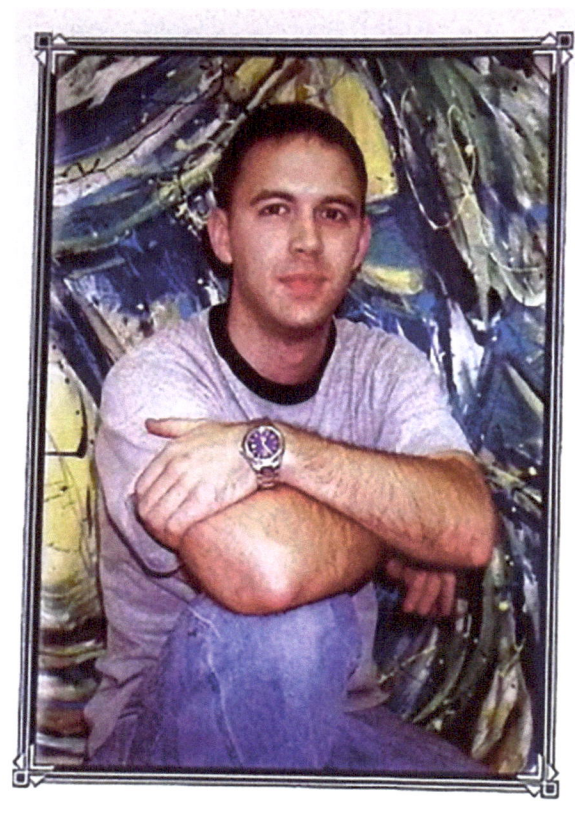

Hans Geist

About the Illustrator

Hans Geist is a South Louisiana artist who graduated from high school in 1994, enrolled at Nicholls State University, and received a Bachelor of Art degree in 2000.

Although his studies were in graphic design, his real passion is for painting and illustration. Starting his own business as a freelance artist, Hans states, "After only three years, God blessed me with Imagine This, a large studio-gallery located in the heart of downtown Houma, Louisiana. God has finally brought me to a place that I am free to express my artwork at age 27 in awesome ways. I thank the Lord daily for the abilities, gifts, and visions that He entrusts in me, for rescuing me, and for giving me a new life."

Geist considers his work as a south Louisiana artist both a blessing and an adventure, is honored to work with Author Chris Billiot on this book, and looks forward to working on more Billiot books in the future

The current illustration featured in this edition is an enhanced version of Hans Geist's original artwork created for the first edition of this book. All enhanced illustrations are fully inspired by Hans' original vision, staying true to his unique artistic style and heartfelt expression.

Personal Invitation

If you have not received Jesus as your personal Savior, I would like you to have a look at the following scriptures taken from the Word of God. I know from the bottom of my heart that once you read them and believe in your heart your life will never be the same:

John 3:16 For God so loved the world, that He have his only begotten Son, that whomever believes in Him should not perish but have everlasting life.

Yes, God gave the best of Heaven so that you and I could live forever in his presence by simply putting our faith in the work that Christ did at the Cross. God sent his Son into the world knowing the whole time the cruel and humiliating death He would endure. That, my friend, proves how much God loves you.

Revelations 3:20 Behold, I Stand at the door and knock. If anyone hears My Voice and open the door, I will come into him and dine with him, and he with Me.

The door that Jesus stands at is your heart. The Savior honors your choice of free will. He will not force Himself into your life. He will only enter your life if you invite Him in.

Revelations 20:12 And I saw the dead, small and great, standing before God, and the books were opened. And another book was opened, which is, "The Book of Lire" and the dead were judged according to their works, by the things which were written in the books.

Revelations 20:15 And anyone not found written in the "Book of Lire" was cast into the lake of fire.

There is a mention of a "Book of Life" in Heaven which lists the names of all saved persons. If you accomplish nothing else in life, be sure to have your name entered into the "Book of Life."

Revelations 21:3 And I heard a loud voice from Heaven saying "behold the Tabernacle of God is with men, and He will dwell with them and they shall be His people. God Himself will be with them and be their God.

Revelations 21:4 And. God will wipe away e very tear from their eyes. There shall be no more death, nor sorrow, nor crying, There shall be no more pain for the former things have passed away.

They have to be the most comforting words anyone can hear. To know that the Almighty cares enough for each and every one of us that he will wipe away our every tear. God desires to dwell among His creation, how honored we should feel. Last but not least, we shall be freed from the fear of death, which cannot exist were. God dwells because God hates death as much as or more than we do, because of the suffering it causes His creation.

Romans 10:19 That if you confess with your mouth Lord Jesus and believe in your heart that God raised Him from the dead you will be saved.

Romans 10:10 For with the heart one believes unto righteousness and with the mouth confession is made unto salvation.

If you believe these words and come to God with the innocence of a child, you can have your name written in "The Book of Life", sometimes called "The Lamb's Book of Life." These scriptures ensure us that God has a plan for the salvation of our souls. He explains it in the simplest terms because God Wishes that no one should perish, but that all should come to the Salvation Knowledge of Jesus Christ. If you desire to be saved and wish to have your name entered into "The Book of Life", please pray the following prayer and mean it will all your heart.

Dear God, I know I am a sinner and that I am lost without the shed blood of Christ to cleanse me. Please, forgive me for my sins and Jesus please come into my heart and life.

What now Seek to be baptized and to belong to a Christ led Church where fellowship with fellow believers and the study of God's Word is essential to your spiritual growth. If you have prayed this prayer in earnest, please let someone know by contacting the following email addresses so that we may rejoice with you in your decision to be a follower of Christ and so that we may pray with you and continually lift you up in prayer.

ccbilliot@aol.com

Reader Comments:

"I am overwhelmed with emotions... We all need to realize how important prayer and peace are."

— *Michelle Pininger*

"I truly believe the story is going to hit the charts... my goodness, it sure was great. I had chill bumps as I read on..."

— *Dawn Harmon*

"I am awe-struck by the words given to you to share. I felt as if I was the person in the story, standing on the balcony and then in the throne room... In all my years of reading, I have never felt such a part of a story before in my life. I was moved to tears and was prompted to reevaluate my walk with my Lord and Savior."

— *Trina Payne*

"The Lord has blessed you with more than a talent for writing. Your story is very powerful, will touch many lives... It opened my eyes. My life will never be the same again."

— *Mrs. E.*

"The story is simple enough for a casual reader to understand, and at the same time, it has an underlying depth and symbolism that will challenge even the most mature Christians. Chris' writing style is so descriptive that the story comes alive, and you feel as if you are a participant in the drama as it unfolds on the pages before you... a must-read for all ages."

— *Marcell Mcgee*